Original title:
In the Tropic's Embrace

Copyright © 2025 Creative Arts Management OÜ
All rights reserved.

Author: Colin Harrington
ISBN HARDBACK: 978-1-80581-681-2
ISBN PAPERBACK: 978-1-80581-208-1
ISBN EBOOK: 978-1-80581-681-2

Dreams on the Horizon

A crab wore a hat, quite absurd,
It danced on the shore, full of spurred.
The seagulls all laughed, what a sight,
A crustacean's ball, oh what a night!

The sun made a splash, like a dive,
Fish in tuxedos, feeling alive.
They wiggled and wobbled, in grand display,
In dreams of the sea, they twirled all day.

Sunsets of Endless Colors

The sky threw a party, shades like a clown,
Orange and pink in a swirling gown.
Clouds in a conga, all dancing tight,
Twirling their ruffles, what a delight!

A flamingo slipped, lost in the hue,
Landed on llamas, oh, what a view!
They giggled and tumbled, all in a row,
As the sunset bowed, putting on a show.

The Kiss of the Salted Wind

The breeze brought whispers, tales from afar,
It tickled my nose, like a candy bar.
A seahorse in shades, sipped a cool drink,
While starfish debated, how to blink!

With laughter and bubbles, it swirled around,
The wind told a joke, almost profound.
But just as I grasped, it vanished away,
Left me with sand, and laughter's bouquet.

Serenade of the Coconut Trees

Coconuts crooned, a tropical song,
Their husky voices sang all night long.
With each gentle sway, they tapped their feet,
In rhythms of laughter, they felt the beat.

Monkeys clapped hands, joining the jam,
In an orchestra sweet, where no one gave a damn.
Bananagrams tossed, words flew so high,
Under the stars, with a wink of an eye.

A Tapestry of Petals and Waves

The sun burnt bright on my funny hat,
A crab tried to steal my fancy mat.
Flowers danced with the tickling breeze,
While I chased them, they laughed with ease.

Shells sang songs of the ocean's pride,
A fish donned shades, looking bona fide.
I tripped on a towel, took quite a fall,
The waves just chuckled, they saw it all.

Nights Wrapped in Tropical Mist

The moon sipped a drink, a coconut bash,
While I spilled mine, made quite a splash.
Fireflies twinkled like stars on a spree,
And the palm trees whispered, 'Come dance with me!'

A parrot squawked jokes in the quiet dark,
Each punchline hit with a cheeky spark.
I laughed so hard, my drinks went airborne,
Oh, how I wished this night was reborn!

Where the Sea Meets the Sky

Splashing about, I thought I was cool,
But a wave sneezed, oh what a fool!
Seagulls laughed as I floundered around,
Turning my confidence upside down.

Sunset paints colors like a clown's grin,
While I juggle seashells, trying to win.
The beach hosts a party without any fuss,
You'll find me cracking jokes, quite a plus!

Poetry of the Monsoon Breeze

Raindrops tapped like a playful beat,
Turning the road into muddy sleet.
Umbrellas turned inside out, oh dear!
Laughter erupted, spilling like beer.

Puddles became stages for leaps and bounds,
While we played hopscotch in drenching sounds.
The sky had a giggle, full of delight,
As we danced in storms, oh what a sight!

Notes from a Paradise Lost

A parrot on my shoulder, squawking loud,
Requesting crackers from the crowd.
Sunburnt tourists with no sense of style,
Tripping over sandcastles, oh what a smile!

The beach ball bursts with a 'thud' and a cheer,
Children clamor, 'Now where is our beer?'
Flip-flops flying, a chaotic delight,
As sunburned folks dance into the night.

Threads of Gold in a Coconut Shell

Coconuts roll like bowling balls,
Who knew drinks could lead to falls?
Straws that twirl like gravity forgot,
Every sip's a lesson in hilarity sought!

The coconut's laughing, it knows the scene,
As I spill my drink like a hapless machine.
Gold threads in shells that tease and taunt,
While my friends shuffle like an odd little font.

Fireflies Dancing to Nature's Tune

Fireflies twinkle, a nightly show,
Outshining my phone's flickering glow.
We wave our arms to synchronizing beats,
Stumbling over roots with hilarious feats.

Nature's DJ spins a mix of delight,
While I trip on shadows, surprised at my height.
In this lively dance, I feel so spry,
Until a mosquito buzzes, "Hey, how am I?"

Sunkissed Souls and Wandering Spirits

Souls basking under sunshine's glare,
Next to a palm with an effective stare.
Wandering spirits with drinks in their hands,
Strategizing escapes from beachy bands.

The sun's too bright; we squint and frown,
Chasing our hats as they tumble down.
With laughter as an anchor, we float on by,
Amidst sips of coconut and the gulls that cry.

Nights that Whisper Secrets to the Sea

Under the moon's gentle glow,
Crabs throw a dance, putting on a show.
Fish gossip in bubbles, oh what a style,
As seaweed sways, they flirt with a smile.

The stars twinkle bright, like popcorn on air,
Seagulls complain, 'This night isn't fair!'
The sand slips from toes, a ticklish tease,
While dolphins debate if they'd rather have cheese.

A coconut falls with a thump that's quite grand,
It startled a turtle—now where's his band?
Jellyfish juggle their glowing delight,
As waves laugh along in the cool of the night.

The ocean hums tunes of breezy delight,
Where pirates once danced, now they've lost their sight.
With treasures of laughter, adventures so free,
Let's toast to the ocean, and all its glee!

The Allure of the Untamed Horizon

There's a parrot who squawks, 'Where's my avocado?'
It tries to surf waves, but oh, what a motto!
Bananas debate if they're ripe or too green,
In this cheeky land, life's a funny scene.

The sun stretches wide, like a cat on a beam,
While palms whisper secrets of a tropical dream.
A turtle gifts flip-flops, what a strange plot!
Now beachgoers wobble, but laugh what they've got!

A crab with sunglasses struts stylish and proud,
Chasing after shadows and singing out loud.
In this zany paradise, with laughter we sing,
Where the tide brings stories that tickle and sting.

The horizon calls out, 'Come join in the fun!'
But the sun can't decide if it's done or just begun.
It dips low then bounces, a classic charade,
In this wild, wacky world, let's all be amazed!

Afternoons Bathed in Endless Light

The sun blares down, my ice cream melts,
A seagull swoops, my snack is felt.
I swat at flies, they dance, they tease,
I wish for shade, or a cooling breeze.

My hat's too small, it barely fits,
Sipping coconut, it's hit or miss.
In bright flip-flops, I twirl and trip,
While crabs on the sand laugh and skip.

Gardens of Eden Under Cloudless Skies

Flowers bloom like they're in a race,
Bees buzzing round like they own the place.
A squirrel shuffles with a nut he found,
Dancing on lawns, so proud and unbound.

Lizards bask on rocks, sunbathing kings,
While I chase butterflies on funny swings.
A neighbor's cat gets jealous and pouts,
As I giggle at these floral clouts.

Stars Alight in the Evening Bliss

The stars come out, I grab a snack,
Fireflies flicker, lighting the track.
A bat swoops down, what a silly sight,
Making me jump in the cool of night.

While shadows dance in a playful way,
I trip on my mat, thank goodness for play!
The moon looks down with a cheeky grin,
As I laugh alone, let the fun begin.

Tranquility Found in Monsoon's Embrace

The rain pours down like a wild horse,
Puddles form, it's a splashy course.
I wore my shoes, oh what a blunder,
Now they float like tiny thunder.

Umbrellas pop like mushrooms do,
As kids throw paper boats, just for view.
And while I sip my hot, sweet tea,
A frog leaps past, laughing at me.

Tides of Passion and Tranquility

The waves dance like they know a joke,
While seagulls cackle, wings rotate.
Each splash a playful, ticklish poke,
As if the ocean can't wait to celebrate.

Flip-flops flying, hats in a spin,
The sun grins wide, spreading delight.
Sandcastles wobble, as if in a din,
Waves tease, chase dreams into the night.

The Colorful Winks of Flora

A flower sneezes, pollen takes flight,
While butterflies giggle at the scene.
Colors blushing, oh what a sight,
Nature's jesters, where laughter's routine.

Cacti wear sunglasses, strut with flair,
Palm trees sway, getting their groove.
Blooming like they've not a care,
Petal dances in a sunny move.

Lullabies of the Island Wind

The wind whispers secrets, so cheeky and sly,
Tugging at everyone's hats with a tease.
It tickles the treetops, oh how they sigh,
While palm fronds wave, looking to please.

A hammock sways, trying to take flight,
Laughing at shoes that dare to escape.
Dreams float off, chased by the light,
As the breeze tosses them into a shape.

Raindrops and Revelations

Raindrops tumble like giggles on roofs,
Puddles splash wildly, a splish-splashing spree.
Umbrellas turn inside out, what goofs,
Making even grumps turn into glee.

Clouds cuddle close, forming a team,
Raining down laughter, unexpected fun.
Each droplet whispers a cheeky dream,
Under the drizzle, no one can shun.

Shadows of the Afternoon Light

Sunrise kicks off a playful chase,
Where umbrellas dance in a sunlit space.
Jellyfish wearing hats made of cheese,
Who knew they'd outsmart the buzzing bees?

Coconuts gossiping with the breeze,
Parrots squawking secrets with such ease.
A crab in sunglasses struts with pride,
While the sandcastles giggle, 'Come inside!'

Heartstrings Tied to the Sea

Turtles salsa dance on ocean's floor,
While seaweed waves does the conga more.
Octopus wearing shoes is quite the sight,
As seagulls argue over who takes flight.

A dolphin sings a silly love song,
Coral reefs join in, they hum along.
With every splash, the laughter is free,
Underwater disco, just you and me!

Meditations under the Mango Canopy

Under the mango tree, we lay down,
Dreaming of mangoes wearing a crown.
A squirrel drops nuts, creates a small show,
While ants line up like they're in a row.

The shadows giggle as the branches sway,
Tickled by breezes that come out to play.
Bees buzz a tune, they're the choir here,
As we crack jokes, cheers ring out sincere.

Rhythms of Dusk and Dawn

Morning light winks, 'Time for some fun!'
The crickets tap dance, day's just begun.
Lizards in bow ties strut through the grass,
While butterflies gossip, "Did you see that sass?"

At dusk, the fireflies twinkle like stars,
While frogs hold a party in tiny cars.
A raccoon prances, taking a bow,
The night orchestra plays, let's dance, whoa wow!

Where the Ocean Kisses the Sky

The seagulls squawk in silly tunes,
While surfers dance on jiggly dunes.
A crab in flip-flops scuttles quick,
Searching for snacks, it's quite the trick.

Palm trees sway with a cheeky grin,
As coconuts fall with a loud din.
They bounce and roll like playful sprites,
Making beachgoers giggle in delight.

Laughter of the Lush Greenery

The monkeys swing with utmost flair,
Wearing hats made of jungle air.
They tickle leaves as they pass by,
Causing butterflies to laugh and fly.

A sloth hangs low, moving in slow-mo,
With a smile that steals the whole show.
He winks at friends on branches wide,
While sipping nectar with pure pride.

Melodies of the Rainforest

The frogs drum beats with croaks so loud,
While dancing lizards form a crowd.
With every splash, they create a scene,
Of wiggly tails and limbs so keen.

Parrots chat in colors so bright,
Replaying gossip from morning light.
They chuckle through the canopy's sway,
Spreading joy in this leafy ballet.

Echoes of the Island Dawn

The rooster crows with comic flair,
Startling tourists in their chairs.
He struts around like he owns the place,
With a pecking dance, oh what a grace!

As waves giggle in playful play,
And tikis grin at the break of day,
The breeze whispers jokes from afar,
Causing flip-flops to do the cha-cha!

Twilight Beneath the Mango Tree

Mangoes fall and plop on toes,
A slapstick way to greet the shows.
Monkeys swing while giggles chime,
We dance to rhythms, lost in time.

Fireflies flicker like disco lights,
While crickets join in silly fights.
A parrot squawks a knock-knock joke,
Our laughter rises, like fragrant smoke.

Beneath the boughs, where shadows creep,
We trade tall tales, not losing sleep.
Each story twists, a comical spin,
Who knew mangoes could bring such grins?

So gather round, let the fun unfold,
In the evening's magic, brave and bold.
Underneath the stars, we make our stand,
With fruit-filled dreams and laughter grand.

Heartbeats of the Tropical Night

The moon hangs low, a silver grin,
As frogs croak ballads tuned for sin.
A sloth drifts by, too slow for haste,
While mischief brews, oh what a taste!

A crab in shades struts on the sand,
Claiming the beach as his own land.
Uninvited, he dances right on by,
We all join in, oh me, oh my!

Palm trees sway, a waltz in disguise,
As stars wink down with watchful eyes.
A coconut falls with a thud and a splash,
We jump with squeals, oh what a crash!

Night giggles gently, a playful muse,
With heartbeats quickening in our shoes.
So come along for this joyful ride,
In this nighttime wonder, let joy abide.

Sunlit Secrets of the Bay

The sun spills gold on waters bright,
Fish giggle and dance, what a sight!
A crab in goggles, a swim and a dive,
Around here, the silly truly thrive.

Seagulls squawk and steal our fries,
While we shout back with playful cries.
Sandcastles rise, but soon they fall,
Like dreams of mermaids at the beach ball.

Tanned toes wiggle, slipping on sand,
The hot sun laughs, it has it planned.
We race the tide, victorious screams,
As waves crash down, we burst our seams.

Secrets sung by the soft ocean breeze,
Remind us to laugh, to dance, to tease.
Under sunlit skies, our spirits sway,
In a world where giggles always play.

Dreams Adrift on Gentle Waves

A raft of laughter, we float along,
With fishy friends who hum a song.
The ocean whispers, secrets spill,
While seashells giggle, what a thrill!

Here comes a dolphin, winking sly,
With tricks that make us gasp and sigh.
We toss out snacks, and watch with glee,
As they shower us with splashes free.

Sunburned noses, hats askew,
We chase the breeze, all bright and new.
Waves tumble forth, like foam-filled cheer,
In the salty air, there's naught to fear.

So here we dream, adrift and free,
On gentle waves, just you and me.
With giggles echoing through the day,
We'll sail on joy, come what may.

Elysium Beneath the Stars

Under the moon, we lost our way,
Chasing fireflies that danced and swayed.
With each misstep, we fell on our backs,
Laughter erupted, and so did our snacks.

Palm trees witnessed our silly plight,
As coconuts dropped, oh what a sight!
We tried to catch them, but fell in the sand,
Elysium giggles with a clumsy hand.

Stars winked brightly at our escapade,
As we swirled around in a goofy charade.
On this night, nothing could bring us down,
In our silly world, we wore the crown.

So here's to the stars and the fun that they share,
With friends and snacks and sandy hair.
In laughter we bloom, let the night last long,
As we sway together, a foolish song.

A Symphony of Lapping Waves

With each wave's kiss, a splash so sweet,
We danced on the shore with sandy feet.
A crab scuttled by, stealing our fries,
We shared a buffet, much to our surprise!

The gulls overhead, a chorus of clucks,
Joined in our laughter, with all of their lucks.
A beach ball soared, then flopped by my head,
We couldn't help giggling; just wished it was bread.

Our voices rose high, bubbles popped all around,
Making sweet symphonies without a sound!
With sand in our hair, we chose not to care,
In this crazy concert, fun was our share.

So let's raise a toast, with beach cups in hand,
To lapping waves and our goofy band.
In the rhythm of tides, we sway and we play,
A symphony bright, come join us today!

Embracing the Warm Rain

Clouds rolled in, with a pitter-pat,
We jumped in puddles; how silly, how fat!
Laughter chimed as we danced in the storm,
Oh, to be kids, so free and so warm!

Raindrops on noses, like tickles from fate,
We spun round and round, oh what a state!
With raucous delight, we splashed and we howled,
Nature's slapstick had our joy cowled.

Umbrellas turned upside down in a twist,
Our fashion statement, no one could resist.
We wore our wet t-shirts, like badges of fun,
In the warm rain's grip, we all came undone.

So here's to the rain, our unpredictable friend,
Embracing the warmth, the joy will not end.
With each silly hop, we find our refrain,
In puddles of laughter, we dance in the rain!

Free Spirits of the Island Breeze

With a breeze on our backs and a grin wide as seas,
We flew like kites, oh, high in the trees!
A parrot squawked loudly, it joined in our fun,
While we twirled like tops, shining bright in the sun.

The waves spoke in whispers, urging us near,
"Dance with the currants, show no hint of fear!"
So we leaped and we bounced, like wild little sprites,
In the funny whirl of our jubilant flights.

The sun painted gold on our shimmering skin,
As we chased after dreams with a cheeky grin.
With moments like these, full of zing and of zest,
Our spirits took flight, oh, we're feeling so blessed!

So here's to the breeze, our whimsical lease,
Where laughter runs wild and worries decrease.
With free spirits soaring, together we rise,
In this silly paradise, under clear skies.

Radiant Hearts of Hibiscus

Hibiscus blooms in the sunny light,
Dancing bees take their flight.
Wearing hats made of sweet delight,
They buzz and sip from morn till night.

Sunburned cheeks and laughter shared,
Coconut drinks, all fully prepared.
Silly hats, we are quite impaired,
Who designed this fashion? How dared!

The petals laugh with colors bold,
A garden fashion show unfolds.
Each flower prances, feeling sold,
From red to pink, a sight to behold.

And when the sun begins to set,
The plants start to get quite upset.
"Please don't leave, we're not done yet!"
As they sip on dew, we can bet.

Whispers of the Coconut Grove

Coconuts chatter in the bright green trees,
"Hey buddy, catch this! Oops, watch the breeze!"
Silly squirrels laugh with ease,
As coconuts fall, they tease and wheeze.

Palm fronds wave as if to say,
"Don't take life too seriously, hey!"
With playful pranks, they whirl and sway,
Even monkeys giggle all day.

The sun hangs low, a golden orb,
Bringing mischief we can absorb.
Knocking fruit down with a little probe,
Creating mayhem like in a burb.

At dusk they gather, a coconut crew,
Throwing shade, just for a view.
Swapping tales, every bit true,
While sipping moon juice, it's quite the brew.

Driftwood Dances on the Shoreline

Driftwood jiggles on sandy feet,
As waves teach it a silly beat.
Shells join in, a mariners' treat,
Together they sway, oh what a feat!

The ocean laughs, a bubbling cheer,
"Come join the dance, bring your weird gear!"
Seagulls squawk with raucous jeer,
While crabs cut in, moving near.

Tidal waves spin, doing the twist,
As driftwood takes its chance on the list.
"Do the moonwalk!" they can't resist,
What a party, you should persist!

With sunset paints, the dance floor glows,
As moonbeams shine and the laughter grows.
A nightly show where nobody knows,
Driftwood and waves steal the shows.

Coral Dreams and Lunar Gleams

Coral dreams in the ocean blue,
Sporting pearls that sparkle anew.
Fish in tuxedos swim right through,
Their gala uniforms, a vivid hue.

Moonlight glimmers, making a splash,
As sea turtles join the party, oh what a bash!
Waltzing waves in a luminous clash,
"Don't take my shell!" – they giggle and dash.

Starfish gossip on the sandy floor,
"I heard the dolphin's got moves galore!"
In the coral court, they all adore,
Each groovy swirl, begging for more.

So come dive deep in the laughter's embrace,
Join the coral's joyous race.
Where the moonlight bids each face,
To dance and twirl in a bubbly space.

The Lure of Uncharted Shores

There's a crab with a monocle, quite absurd,
He reads maps while dashing, so very disturbed.
With a compass in hand, he directs a parade,
Of turtles in top hats, all set for charade.

A seagull sings opera atop a tall tree,
But its voice sounds more like a cat with a flea.
The dolphins do tap dance, a splash and a flip,
While the fish form a band, they've all got the grip.

They argue over shells, calling 'dibs' on the best,
While the octopus grumbles, looking quite stressed.
With tentacles flailing, its hat falls away,
The audience is laughing, not a serious day.

So here's to the shores where the laughter is free,
A menagerie of creatures, all wild and silly.
Pack your bags for the beach, let's make some noise,
For the world is alive with the dance of the joys.

Daydreams Stirred by Ocean's Breath

Waves whisper secrets, like a gossiping friend,
They speak of the sandcastles that never quite blend.
A wobbly crab with sunglasses struts on the coast,
Declaring himself king; he's proud, but a host.

The sun loungers snicker at a seagull's dive,
It thought it was graceful; it barely survived!
A flip and a splash, the beachgoers cheer,
As the gull shakes off water—what a comical smear!

A beach ball goes rogue, it rolls down the shore,
Chasing flip-flops like it's seeking out more.
The ice cream is melting, it slips from your hand,
Which brings a loud laugh, oh, isn't it grand?

So daydream away as the beach waves take flight,
With jellyfish waltzing under the sunlight.
Let the humor of waves be a balm for your days,
In this land of delight, let laughter amaze.

Elysian Fields of Marigold and Sea

Golden sands glisten with glittering tease,
While the seashells debate who can tickle like bees.
The crabs are renowned for their dancing ballet,
In tutus made from seaweed—what a wild display!

A flamingo snorts loudly, it thinks it can fly,
But it trips on its legs and flops with a sigh.
The starfish play poker on a surfboard that's bright,
With jellybeans as chips, it's a bizarre sight!

The fish throw a party, a splash in the sun,
With bubbles and giggles, they're having such fun.
A clam in a bowtie serves drinks on the sand,
While the sea cucumbers form a weird band.

In fields where the laughter is easy and loud,
Each creature shares stories, both nutty and proud.
So, roam through this haven, where fun never flees,
Among marigolds golden and shimmering seas.

Ripples of Laughter on the Breeze

A parrot in shades squawks a joke, quite absurd,
While the fish try to chuckle, it sounds a bit blurred.
Crabs play charades, all flailing their claws,
The winners get seaweed, the silliest laws!

As the breeze pulls the laughter, it sweeps by with grace,
Twirling beach towels like they're a dance in a race.
A sand dollar chirps in a voice soft and low,
While the gulls form a choir—oh what a show!

The starfish applaud with their five little hands,
As the buffoons of the tide create chaotic bands.
With surfboards as drums and a sand hut as stage,
The performance gets wild, all creatures engage.

So let every ripple tickle your soul,
With merriment swirling, we'll play like a shoal.
Join in the delight that the ocean conveys,
As we ride on the waves of these laughter-filled days.

Lush Laneways of Paradise

Through winding paths the llamas trot,
With sunglasses on, looking quite hot.
Bananas fall, the monkeys squeal,
In this green maze, who will take the wheel?

Parrots chat and gossip loud,
Dancing freely, oh so proud.
A coconut drops with a thud,
Splattering our picnic—what's the big dud?

Umbrellas flop like fish in air,
As the sun tries, tempting us to dare.
We run and jump, try to explore,
But end up tangled behind the door!

As the day ends and fireflies spark,
A crab plays music, just as we'd hark.
In paradise, with laughter's trace,
We'll waddle home, oh what a race!

The Scent of Sea and Sand

Breezy air, a smell so grand,
A mix of salt and sunscreen hand.
Seagulls squawk, they've come for snacks,
Watch your sandwich, they'll stage an attack!

Sandcastles rise, but what a mess,
Where's the moat? Oh, what distress!
While kids build kingdoms, fate mocks them,
A wave crashes in—hello, here comes mayhem!

Tongues of ice cream drip and slide,
We yell, 'It's melting!' and run to hide.
With chocolate sprinkles, we start to cheer,
Only to find ants are now near!

As sunset falls, we sit and dine,
Feasting on laughter, and a bit of brine.
With every bite, we reminisce,
In the scent of joy, what a bliss!

Footprints on the Golden Coast

Barefoot adventures, we race the tide,
Each footprint made, oh what a slide!
Sandy toes and salty cheek,
Chasing crabs—how fast they sneak!

Shells as treasures, we gather with glee,
This one's a hat! Can you see me?
Boogie boards roll like surfboards lost,
We launch ourselves—guess the cost?

Sunburns bloom like flowers bright,
'Twas a fun day but oh, what a fright!
With aloe slathered, we shriek and laugh,
In sun-soaked joy, we find our path.

As shadows grow long and evening sways,
We chat about our silly blunders and plays.
With footprints fading, we giggle and dance,
At day's end, we'll try our luck at romance!

Melodies of the Coral Reef

Beneath the waves, the fish do sway,
In a rhythm we can't quite play.
Crabs do tango with anemones,
While dolphins laugh, oh how they tease!

A starfish hums a soft refrain,
With seaweed dancers joining in the lane.
Clownfish wearing bow ties fancy,
Swipe the show, how very chancy!

Turtles glide with style supreme,
Swimming past us, oh what a dream!
With bubbles bursting like tiny balloons,
The concert ends, where's the marooned?

Back on the shore, we'll share a smile,
With memories made—stay a while!
In this underwater groove so free,
We find our place, on the coral spree!

Serene Shores and Shimmering Dreams

Seagulls squawk their morning tune,
While crabs do the cha-cha by the moon.
Flip-flops fly with an airy grace,
As tourists trip in this sandy place.

Children giggle, they build and splash,
While sunscreen turns into a sticky mash.
Wave after wave, a frosty treat,
Who knew sandcastles could taste so sweet?

Old men nap in a sun-kissed haze,
While ice cream drips in a sugary daze.
Shells whisper secrets from the deep,
But those ice cubes are making me weep!

As sunsets paint the sky with flair,
The seashore dances without a care.
With laughter mingling in the breeze,
Who needs a fence when you've got these?

Dance of the Palm Fronds

Palms sway gently in the breeze,
Looking for a dance partner, oh please!
A coconut drops with a mighty thud,
Palms look shocked—what a nutty dud!

Swaying to tunes from the strangest bands,
With tiny crabs casting jazzy strands.
Belly laughing beneath the sun,
Even the lizards join in the fun!

Bees buzz about with a sticky plan,
Trying to steal a sip from the pan.
While the sun gives visitors a sunburn,
It's all in good jest—they'll surely learn!

With goofy grins and awkward feet,
The palm fronds wobble to the beat.
In a world where humor's the dress code,
The lighthearted laughter will lighten the load!

Beneath the Radiant Canopy

Under a ceiling of vibrant glee,
Squirrels play hide and seek with a bee.
Leaves drop down like confetti confound,
As the ground squirrels spin round and round.

Lizards strut in their bright little shoes,
Showing off colors that dare not lose.
Under the shade, a picnic sprawls wide,
Until a sandwich rolls off with pride!

Frogs crack jokes as they jump on logs,
While butterflies flirt with the old fat dogs.
Banana peels slip to aid the show,
Letting out snickers from the tree's low bow.

As the sunlight filters with perfect charm,
Every creature finds a way to disarm.
In this world of whimsy and ease,
Humor's the heart under the green leaves!

Echoes of the Ocean's Breath

Waves roll in with a comical crash,
Fish try jumping, but just belly-flash.
A beach ball soars like a bird on the run,
Only to land right where the hermits have fun!

Starfish grumble in the salty spray,
"I can't walk straight; I'm having a day!"
A dolphin pops up with a fishy grin,
Saying, "Hey buddy, let's take a spin!"

Surfers glide but trip on a swell,
Spinning and splashing— oh, what the hell!
Sand sticks to legs like a clown's big shoes,
Laughing at woes while picking their blues.

As seashells whisper tales from afar,
Each ocean wave brings a new bizarre.
The giggles echo, riding the tide,
With pure joy as the ocean's guide!

The Dance of Vibrant Flora

Beneath the sun, flowers spin,
They wave their petals, cheeky grin.
A daisy winks, a rose takes a bow,
While orchids laugh, 'Look at me now!'

The breeze joins in, a partner bold,
Swirling around, stories unfold.
With every sway, a giggle bursts,
As bees come buzzing, craving their thirst.

Petals pirouette on a joyful spree,
While the gardener hums, sipping his tea.
"Keep it down!" the butterfly shouts,
"Your raucous dance has too many clouts!"

But the garden giggles, blooms in a whirl,
In nature's fun, they happily twirl.
Each leaf and stem takes part in the jest,
For life in full color is truly the best!

Rhythms of the Coastal Tide

Waves come crashing with a playful sound,
While crabs in pajamas dart all around.
Seagulls crack jokes in a feathery band,
As fish joke back from their watery land.

The tide rolls in, then it rolls out,
Shells wear grins, there's no room for doubt.
"Did you hear that?" a clam starts to yell,
"I saw a wave that tickled a shell!"

Fishermen chuckle with their nets all caught,
Tropical sun gives a sting that's hot.
"I'm here for dinner!" a dolphin will plead,
"Just one more jig before I take the lead!"

As sandcastles tumble, kids all applaud,
With laughter that echoes, the sight they'll applaud.
In this coastal rhythm, joy takes flight,
Where every splash holds a giggly delight!

Fluttering Hues of the Tropical Bird

In a colorful flash, they flit and they sway,
Feathers so bright, they brighten the day.
Parrots gossip, they squawk and they squabble,
While toucans debate if they're cool, or just wobble.

"Oh look at me!" cries a bird in the breeze,
"I can do tricks, I can do these!"
While hummingbirds dash in a buzzing spree,
"Who's faster now? Is it you or just me?"

A flock takes a selfie, it's all in good fun,
With plumage catching rays of the tropical sun.
Each snap brings a giggle, each flutter a cheer,
As the jungle joins in with a raucous jeer.

They play hide and seek in the leaves up high,
Every time they peek, there's a comical cry.
In the trees the laughter becomes a sweet tune,
As birds paint the sky under the bright moon!

The Scent of Hibiscus and Sea

Hibiscus wears a crown, bright pink and bold,
Noses wiggle with scents of the stories untold.
A sniff here, a puff there, it's quite a delight,
"Is that mango or guava? Oh, it smells just right!"

The breeze brings whispers of salts and of blooms,
"Hey check out my flower!" a bold little plume.
"Did you hear what the turtle said today?"
"Something about pasta!" oh, what a cliché!

The ocean giggles, waves crashing with flair,
While the sun winks down, teasing with glare.
"Smell that?" says the coconut, full of glee,
"It's not just the flowers, it's the taste of me!"

Laughter mingles in the sweet salty air,
Each whiff tells a tale, no need for a dare.
In this fragrant dance, joy finds a way,
Mixing hibiscus and sea, come what may!

The Silence Between the Crickets

Crickets chirp with great delight,
Yet one forgot his lines tonight.
The frogs are laughing, what a scene,
While he just sits, a lost machine.

The moon is bright, the breeze is sly,
Our friend the cricket starts to cry.
He lifts his legs with all his might,
But still can't find the words to light.

A ladybug rolls by with cheer,
"Just hum along, my friend, no fear!"
But cricket's stuck like glue on gum,
Just waiting for that big ole drum.

So let us toast to all the sounds,
Though one of them has lost the grounds.
In silence now, he may regret,
The funniest night he can't forget.

Journey to the Heart of the Lagoon

We set our sails for waters bright,
To find the fish that spark at night.
But Gary's boat is full of holes,
His plans for fun have sunken goals.

A pelican joins in the game,
Diving for fish, but missing fame.
With every splash, we burst in glee,
As Gary swims, fish tease from sea.

An octopus waves with eight bright arms,
He knows how to avoid the harms.
But Gary grabs, and what a mess,
He hugs it tight, then feels the stress.

With seaweed hair and salty grin,
Our journey's not about to win.
But laughter rings as waters sway,
In the lagoon, we'll splash and play.

Sunsets Weaving Tales of Gold

The sun dips low, a golden show,
But Auntie Jo forgot to sew.
Her dress is stuck, it looks a sight,
As colors blend, it's quite the fright.

The clouds are draped in peachy hues,
While she tries hard to pick her shoes.
"Oh, look! A duck with style and flair,"
But duck just honks, doesn't care.

As twilight dances, Auntie twirls,
In mismatched shoes and glittered pearls.
A sunset blooms, it steals the scene,
While her fashion dreams are torn at the seam.

Yet laughter fills the evening air,
With friends and quirks beyond compare.
So raise your glass to sunset's gold,
And quirky tales that never get old.

Symphony of the Starry Night

The stars are twinkling, cats all howling,
But here's a dog, he seems quite bowing.
He thinks he's part of this grand band,
With every bark, he missed the stand.

A pig on drums, a cow on keys,
They jam so loud, it shakes the trees.
Yet Fido tries to steal the show,
With every woof, he steals the flow.

A comet zooms, all eyes will stare,
But it's the dog that steals the air.
He jumps and spins, a jolly sight,
Keep time, dear pup, with all your might!

So stars and moon get lost in cheer,
With laughter loud that none will fear.
Together they make music bright,
In this symphony of the starry night.

Currents of the Emerald Waters

Fish in shorts with shades so bright,
They swim around, a silly sight.
A turtle slow, with a beach ball,
He challenges all, to a race call.

Crabs dance sideways, on the sand,
With tiny moves, they make a band.
They pinch the toes of passing feet,
Their happy tunes can't be beat.

A dolphin leaps, with joyful glee,
He steals a drink from my Piña Colada, you see!
Splashing water all over the bar,
I think he's had one too many, bizarre!

The mangoes fall from the trees above,
Like nature's kiss of a sweet, warm love.
They land with a squish, what a fun noise,
The fruit's a prankster, oh what joys!

Reflections in the Lagoon

The mirror of water sparkles and gleams,
I spot a frog with grand disco dreams.
He jumps to the beat of the tunes in my head,
Disco in the swamp, I'd join him instead!

A fish with a wig swirls by with flair,
He's having a party, with no room to spare.
He winks and he twirls, then shows off his moves,
Leaving the other fish with nothing to prove.

The lily pads hold a tea party grand,
With bugs in tuxedos, oh isn't it grand?
Sipping dew drops and munching on leaves,
Gossiping softly, sharing big grieves.

Reflections of laughter ripple with fun,
Splashing each other, they've nowhere to run.
With silly antics, they're quite the crew,
In this lagoon where the laughter just grew!

A Caress of Warmth and Light

Sunbeams tickle my sandy toes,
While I sip on coconut, what joy it bestows.
A parrot perched says, 'You're looking fine!'
I wink back, 'Buddy, your feathers shine!'

Palm trees gossip, swaying with glee,
Sharing secrets, oh, the shade's so free.
They whisper of love and picnic plans,
While sipping on juice from tiny cans.

A crab in a hat struts by with pride,
He waves at the sun, oh, what a ride!
His pinch is friendly, his dance quite absurd,
A crustacean star? That's quite the word!

Warmth hugs me tight, a light-hearted muse,
Nature's been at work, with its playful views.
Each wave that crashes brings laughter anew,
Yes, I'm convinced, this is paradise too!

Threads of Paradise

A hammock swings in a breezy way,
It tells me tales as it rocks to play.
With a side of laughter and beachside snacks,
I'm wrapped up tight in its cozy tracks.

Seashells giggle beneath my feet,
Whispering stories of adventures sweet.
They chatter softly as waves come ashore,
Their joyous voices, I can't ignore.

The monkeys above swing alarmingly wild,
Each vine they grasp, is a chance to be styled.
With mischief in their eyes and snacks in their hands,
I've learned to keep my food close at hand!

When the sun dips low, dusk paints the day,
Fireflies join, as the moon starts to sway.
In this paradise, I'm soaked in delight,
With threads of laughter, stitched all through the night!

Whispers of a Sunlit Breeze

The sunbeams play, they stretch and tease,
As lizards laugh and shake their knees.
A parrot squawks, 'Hey, look at me!'
While flip-flops flop, we dance with glee.

Coconuts roll from trees above,
They drop like bombs on those we love.
A sunburnt nose, a glorious sight,
Though sunscreen applied, it missed a bite!

The breeze is cheeky, a playful swish,
It lifts our hats, a windy wish.
We chase the hats with silly cheer,
While sandcastles tumble, that's our fear!

Bikini tops are flying high,
A crab scuttles quick, oh my, oh my!
In laughter's grip, we find our place,
The fun unfolds with each sunlit trace.

Dance of the Palm Fronds

The palms sway gently, like they're grooving,
With tiny critters, barely moving.
A chubby squirrel prances with flair,
While sipping nectar without a care.

The coconut crew are up to no good,
Rolling in the sun like they think they should.
While tourists slip on slippery ground,
The laughter echoes, a joyous sound.

The beach ball bounces, oh what a scene,
As kids chase after, quick and keen.
A seagull swoops, with a honk so loud,
Stealing a chip from a nearby crowd.

Cactus drinks in shades of fun,
We all agree, it beats a gun!
With palm fronds dancing, we join the play,
In a carnival of sun, come what may!

Beneath the Mango Canopy

Mangoes drop down with a juicy plop,
While laughter bounces like a cheerful bop.
A kid slips down, with a gleeful scream,
While the neighbors wave, but it's just a dream!

The shadows play tricks as we all meet,
A furry raccoon steals leftover treat.
Running around in zigzag delight,
As moonlight dances all through the night.

A hammock swings, it's a carnival ride,
Where sleepy heads bob and giggles collide.
A cat gets tangled in ropes and care,
As all of us shout, 'Hey, did we share?'

Beneath the mango, we huddle tight,
Counting each star, under soft moonlight.
With silly banter, our hearts all soar,
In this goofy glade, who could want more?

Secrets of the Coral Shore

On the coral carpet, we make a scene,
With flip-flops flopping, we're quite the machine.
A crab gives chase, with a comical scare,
As we giggle loud without a care.

Seashells whisper their tales of old,
Of pirate treasure, of shining gold.
But all we find is a sock and a shoe,
And we laugh out loud, 'Is this all true?'

A dolphin leaps with a joyful squeal,
While we attempt to swim, but let's be real.
Flailing like fish, we make a splash,
With heaps of laughter, the moment's a dash.

Secrets untold in the salty spray,
We toss back jokes as the sun fades away.
With sand in our toes and hearts full of lore,
We'll treasure this day forever, once more!

Unfurling Leaves of Desire

Green fronds giggle in the breeze,
Palm trees dance, waving with ease.
Coconuts drop with a splat on the ground,
Nature's laughter is often loud.

With each rustle, secrets shared,
Frogs wear sunglasses, feeling quite scared.
A lizard chats with a passing bee,
In this green world, all's wild and free.

Flowers chuckle as the sun climbs high,
It's a colorful circus beneath the sky.
Bees do the tango, buzzing along,
Every moment here feels like a song.

Butterflies flutter, in riotous hues,
Daring to dance in their fancy shoes.
With smiles so bright, they paint the air,
Life's a joyride, without a care.

The Gaze of the Setting Sun

The sun slips down in a playful way,
Painting skies in orange and gray.
Crabs hold hands, prancing on sand,
While tourists slip on sunscreen, unplanned.

Parrots squawk their evening tunes,
As if rehearsing for cartoonish cartoons.
A dog chases waves, with waggling tail,
The ocean chuckles; it's a laughing gale.

The horizon blushes, what a sight to see,
Seagulls argue over a crumb of brie.
Friends sip drinks with umbrellas so bright,
While sunsets glow—what a silly delight!

"Goodnight!" says the sun, "Till we meet again!"
Stars start to twinkle, a cheeky grin.
As darkness settles, the world's aglow,
In this whimsical hour, who wouldn't know?

Echoes Beneath the Banyan Tree

Under the branches, shadows play,
Whispers of mischief glide away.
Squirrels debate on the best nut stash,
While a sleeping cat dreams of a flash.

Lizards lie lazy, on sun-warmed bark,
While ants march in a comic arc.
A parrot critiques, a wannabe sage,
In this grand theater, everyone's on stage.

Banyan roots tangle, a merry snare,
Hiccups from laughter drift through the air.
The breeze tells jokes, fluttering leaves,
Sharing stories that no one believes.

As dusk arrives with a whimsical hue,
The tree hums tunes, both old and new.
Life here is funny, a grand charade,
Under the banyan, adventures are made.

A Dream Built on Silken Sands

Soft sands whisper secrets untold,
Where beach umbrellas flop in bold.
Kids build castles that rival the skies,
While seagulls steal fries, oh what a surprise!

Waves race forth like mischief-makers,
Chasing footprints of sunbathers and fakers.
A crab scuttles by in a tuxedoed suit,
Pretending to be royalty, oh what a hoot!

Beach balls float on a sea of cheer,
As laughter bubbles with every beer.
A sunburned tourist, red as a rose,
Sits muttering tales of adventures he knows.

As nighttime falls, the stars start to wink,
While dolphins leap, teasing us to think.
Dreams are woven in grains of gold,
In this funny paradise, let life unfold!

Serenity Found in Seaswept Lands

The crab did a dance, in a conga line,
With seaweed hats, oh how they shine!
A dolphin dove by, took a selfie too,
Waving hello, as if it knew.

Sandcastles toppled by the laughing tide,
Seashells giggled while they tried to hide.
A beach ball bounced, chased by a breeze,
"Life's a party!" yelled a bird in the trees.

The Allure of the Untamed Coast

A parrot squawked tales of high seas fears,
While tourists dropped ice cream in their cheers.
Sharks in sunglasses swim past so cool,
While jellyfish jiggle like they're at school.

Seagulls gossip, causing an uproar,
Stealing fries from a child, oh what a chore!
A lone fisherman sings with a hook in hand,
"Reel in the laughter, it's all part of the plan!"

Candles of Light in the Night Wind

Balloons in the air, looking for friends,
A lantern gets loose, on whiffing winds bends.
A sparkler winks, with a cheeky glow,
While fireflies flicker, putting on a show.

Mermaids chuckle, flipping their tails,
As sailors share stories over beer-filled pails.
The stars all giggle, a million winks,
"Just look at those folks, don't you think they stink?"

Silhouettes Against a Fiery Sky

Shadows stretch out like they forgot their backs,
As surfers ride waves with ridiculous hacks.
The sunset is painting funny faces gold,
While a cat on a beach towel looks mighty bold.

Footprints in sand tell tales of the day,
One pair's lost, pointing the wrong way.
Laughter erupts as a kid does a flop,
Sunset chimes in, "That's the best, never stop!"

www.ingramcontent.com/pod-product-compliance
Lightning Source LLC
Chambersburg PA
CBHW072133070526
44585CB00016B/1664